GUINNESS WGUINNESS WORLD RECORDSRLD RECORDS

BOOK OF
ULTIMATE
RECORDS

COLLECT & COMPARE WITH

GUINNESS WORLD RECORDS

FEARLESS FEATS
Incredible Records of Human Achievement

WILD LIVES
Outrageous Animal & Nature Records

JUST OUTRAGEOUS
Extraordinary Records of Unusual Facts & Feats

DEADLY DISASTERS
Catastrophic Records in History

MYSTERIES & MARVELS OF THE PAST
Historical Records of Phenomenal Discoveries

BIGGEST, TALLEST, GREATEST!
Records of Overwhelming Size

GUINNESS W✪RLD RECORDS

BOOK OF ULTIMATE RECORDS

Compiled by Kris Hirschmann and Ryan Herndon

For Guinness World Records:
Jennifer Osborne, Laura Barrett Plunkett,
Craig Glenday, Stuart Claxton, Michael Whitty,
and Laura Jackson

SCHOLASTIC INC.
New York   Toronto   London   Auckland   Sydney
Mexico City   New Delhi   Hong Kong   Buenos Aires

Guinness World Records Limited has a very thorough accreditation system for records verification. However, while every effort is made to ensure accuracy, Guinness World Records Limited cannot be held responsible for any errors contained in this work. Feedback from our readers on any point of accuracy is always welcomed.

© 2008 Guinness World Records Limited

Published by Scholastic Inc. SCHOLASTIC and associated logos are trademarks and/or registered trademarks of Scholastic Inc.

ISBN-13: 978-0-439-10485-2
ISBN-10: 0-439-10485-8

Designed by Scholastic Art Department
Photo Research by Els Rijper
Records from the Archives of Guinness World Records

12 11 10 9 8 7 6 5 4 3 2   8 9 10 11/0

Printed in the U.S.A.

First printing, November 2008

Visit Guinness World Records at www.guinnessworldrecords.com

CONTENTS

The idea for Guinness World Records grew out of a question. In 1951, Sir Hugh Beaver, the managing director of the Guinness Brewery, wanted to know which was the fastest game bird in Europe — the golden plover or the grouse? Some people argued that it was the grouse. Others claimed it was the plover. A book to settle the debate did not exist until Sir Hugh discovered the knowledgeable twin brothers Norris and Ross McWhirter, who lived in London.

Like their father and grandfather, the McWhirter twins loved information. They were kids when they started clipping interesting facts from newspapers and memorizing important dates in world history. As well as learning the names of every river, mountain range, and nation's capital, they knew the record for pole squatting (196 days in 1954), which language had only one irregular verb (Turkish), and that the grouse — flying at a timed speed of 43.5 miles per hour — is faster than the golden plover at 40.4 miles per hour.

Norris and Ross served in the Royal Navy during World War II, graduated from college, and launched their own fact-finding business called McWhirter Twins, Ltd. They were the perfect people to compile the book of records that Sir Hugh Beaver searched for yet could not find.

The first edition of *The Guinness Book of Records* was published on August 27, 1955, and since then has been published in 37 languages and more than 100 countries. In 2000, the book title changed to *Guinness World Records* and has set an incredible record of its own: Excluding non-copyrighted books such as the Bible and the Koran, *Guinness World Records* is the best-selling book of all time!

Today, the official Keeper of the Records keeps a careful eye on each Guinness World Record, compiling and verifying the greatest the world has to offer — from the fastest and tallest to the slowest and the smallest, with everything in between.

INTRODUCTION

The *Ultimate* Thrill Ride!

For more than 50 years, Guinness World Records has measured, weighed, timed, verified, and documented the world's ultimate record-breakers in every category imaginable. Today, the records in their archives number more than 40,000.

In this collection, we analyze 23 opposing pairs that represent the extremes of their fields. We'll ride high on the tallest living horse, then lean *waaaay* down to pet the smallest one. We'll explore the world's highest mountains and deepest ocean trenches. We'll also walk through fire and swim under ice!

This book takes you on the ultimate thrill ride — whether you're sitting in a chair or standing on your head. All you have to do is turn the page to read the inspiring and incredible stories behind the history-making facts.

CHAPTER 1

Creatures Big and Small

Mother Nature grows them in all sizes, from tiny to tremendous! In this chapter, you'll gaze upon super-sized dogs, horses, salamanders, and monkeys, then smile at their itsy-bitsy counterparts. Big or small, these amazing animals have one thing in common: They're all record- breakers. Get ready to meet the entire menagerie on the ultimate Guinness World Records safari!

Largest Amphibian

Record Holder:	Chinese giant salamander
Place:	China

Watch your step when wading in the mountain streams of northeastern, central, and southern China. You may trip over the **Largest Amphibian** (pictured)! The Chinese giant salamander *(Andrias davidianus)* can grow up to 5 feet, 11 inches long, and weigh over 140 pounds. A typical specimen is smaller; the average for this species is around 45 inches and 25 pounds. These creatures spend their entire lives underwater, resting in comfortable hollows on the streambed. They maintain their huge bodies with a tasty diet of insects, frogs, and fish.

Smallest Salamander

Record Holder:	Mexican lungless salamander
Place:	Mexico, Belize, and Guatemala

Speaking of diets, it's all about bananas and coffee for the **Smallest Salamander** (pictured). However, the Mexican lungless salamander *(Bolitoglossa mexicana)* doesn't actually eat those items. It lives in the banana groves and coffee plantations of Mexico, Belize, and Guatemala. This little critter measures just 1 inch in length, including the tail, when fully grown. That's about the size of a human thumb's tip. As its name suggests, this salamander doesn't have lungs. It is so small that it can absorb all the oxygen it needs through its paper-thin skin.

ULTIMATE FACTS

The Chinese giant salamander is critically endangered, which means it has an extremely high risk of becoming extinct. The population drop is mostly due to overhunting. People catch these oversized amphibians and sell them to restaurants, where they are cooked and served as gourmet snacks.

ULTIMATE FACTS

The Mexican lungless salamander is considered a "Least Concern" species. This means its population appears to be healthy. However, these animals are much less common than they used to be. Their population is shrinking because people have destroyed many of the forests where they used to live.

Largest Monkey

Record Holder: Mandrill

Place: West Africa

Male mandrills are brightly colored to attract females. See their spectacular coats in this book's color photo section.

A full-grown mandrill can outweigh a human, and that's no monkey business! Found in equatorial West Africa, the male mandrill *(Mandrillus sphinx)* has an average head and body length of 24 to 30 inches and a tail length of 2 to 3 inches. Most mandrills tip the scales around the 55-pound mark, but a male can weigh in at 120 pounds, making it the **Largest Monkey**. These animals often form large clans. Scientists once found 1,300 mandrills living together. You'd need a lot of monkey bars to entertain *that* gigantic group!

Smallest Monkey

ULTIMATE FACTS

Camouflage is the pygmy marmoset's main defense against predators. Its light brown and gray fur with yellow and green highlights help it blend into its treetop habitat.

Record Holder: Pygmy marmoset
Place: South America

How could the **Smallest Monkey** have a tail longer than its mighty mandrill cousin? The pygmy marmoset (*Callithrix pygmaea*) averages only 5.35 inches from nose to rear, and weighs between 4 and 5 ounces (pictured). But its tail can be nearly 8 inches long! Pygmy marmosets live in the forests of South America's Amazon Basin (Peru, Ecuador, Colombia, Bolivia, and Brazil). Strong legs help the pygmy marmoset jump between tree branches and even leap more than 16 feet straight up into the air!

Record Holder:	Thumbelina
Date:	July 7, 2006
Place:	Missouri, USA

A miniature sorrel brown mare, Thumbelina is about the size of a medium house dog. Appropriately, she sleeps in a dog house instead of a horse stall! This tiny trotter earned the title of **Smallest Living Horse** in July 2006, when she was officially measured at just 17.5 inches tall. Owned by Kay and Paul Goessling of St. Louis, Missouri, USA, Thumbelina does big work with her small body. Similar to a therapy dog, Thumbelina's job is to visit sick, needy, and disabled children in her role as spokeshorse for the Thumbelina Charitable Foundation. That's a big job for such a little horse!

Flip to this book's special color photo section to see how tiny Thumbelina measures up next to giant Radar, the title-holder of Tallest Living Horse.

Tallest Living Horse

Record Holder:	Radar
Date:	July 27, 2004
Place:	Ontario, Canada

When riding on the **Tallest Living Horse**, you need a bridle, reins, a saddle, and a ladder (pictured)! A Belgian draft horse named Radar became the Guinness World Record-holder during the North American Belgian Championship held in London, Ontario, Canada, on July 27, 2004. Official measurements found Radar to stand 19 hands 3.5 inches tall. How high is that? A Hummer vehicle at 73.7 inches is smaller than this horse at 79.5 inches. Plus, horses are measured from the shoulder down to the hooves, meaning Radar is even taller from hoof to head in height.

ULTIMATE FACTS

Radar weighs 2,400 pounds. How does he stay healthy? His owners at Priefert Manufacturing, Inc. in Mount Pleasant, Texas, fork over a lot of hay. Radar eats 40 pounds of hay, 18 pounds of grain and drinks 20 gallons of water each day.

ULTIMATE FACTS

Thumbelina weighs just 58 pounds. By bulk, you could squeeze nearly 42 horses of this size into the area occupied by Radar! Thumbelina has a small appetite to go with her tiny body. Twice a day, the miniature mare satisfies her hunger with one cup of oats and a handful of hay.

Tallest Living Dog

Record Holder:	Gibson
Date:	August 31, 2004
Place:	California, USA

Check out this book's cover photo to see the height difference between these canine champions.

All Great Danes are big. But a harlequin Great Dane named Gibson is unquestionably the top dog! This prodigious pooch measures 42.2 inches at the shoulder. Up on his hind legs, Gibson tops the 7-foot mark. With numbers like these, it's no wonder Gibson holds the Guinness World Record as the **Tallest Living Dog**. Owned by Sandy Hall of Grass Valley, California, USA, Gibson puts his bulk to good use every day in his job as a therapy dog. "He just puts a smile on people's faces," says his doting owner.

ULTIMATE FACTS

Therapy dogs visit hospitals, retirement homes, and schools. Their job is to let people hug and pet them, and to give lots of love in return.

Smallest Living Dog

Record Holder:	Boo Boo
Date:	May 12, 2007
Place:	Kentucky, USA

Does your taste run to pint-sized pups? If so, a Chihuahua named Boo Boo may be your cup of tea. On May 12, 2007, this long-haired female earned the title of **Smallest Living Dog** by measuring exactly 4 inches tall at the shoulder. How small is that? Gibson's tongue is about the length of Boo Boo's doggie bed! Owned by Lana Elswick of Raceland, Kentucky, USA, Boo Boo was the size of a human thumb at birth. She reached her current size around her first birthday, when she became eligible for Guinness World Records consideration.

ULTIMATE FACTS

Don't laugh the next time you see a petite pooch in a sweater. It's harder for small dogs to stay warm.

A Breed Apart

Owner Sandy Hall knows her dog Gibson is a real standout in his breed (pictured). How did he get so tall? Although all Great Danes are tall and all Chihuahuas are small, the size difference didn't happen by itself. It is the result of hundreds of years of careful breeding. To create a new dog breed, people find dogs with traits they like and encourage them to have puppies. The puppies inherit their parents' features. When the puppies become adults, the breeders choose the most promising ones and repeat the process. Over many generations, the desired features — such as tallness or shortness — become more and more pronounced.

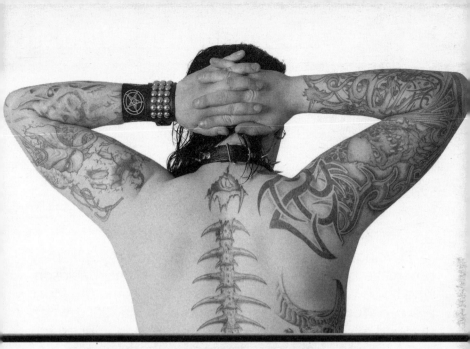

CHAPTER 2

Fabulous Folks

In every group, there seems to be one person who takes things to the extreme! Guinness World Records has seen it all, and in this chapter we spotlight some favorite human record-holders. You'll get poked and prodded by a pair of body art aficionados, stand eye-to-eye with the tallest living man and woman, and explore space with history's youngest and oldest astronauts. It's individuality at its finest!

Most Pierced Woman

Record Holder:	Elaine Davidson
Date:	May 2000
Place:	Edinburgh, Scotland

See Elaine's shining personality on display in this book's color photo section!

Piercings aren't as permanent as tattoos. Still, they can make quite a statement. Just ask Elaine Davidson, who holds the Guinness World Record for being the **Most Pierced Woman**. Elaine earned her title in May 2000, when she had 462 piercings. Today, this human pincushion has 4,225 metal objects adorning her body! A native of Brazil, Elaine now lives in Edinburgh, Scotland, where she runs a Brazilian restaurant and amazes patrons with her fabulously bejeweled body.

ULTIMATE FACTS

Fashion isn't for the fearless. The approximate total weight of Elaine Davidson's fabulous body jewelry is an additional six pounds!

Most Tattooed Person

Record Holder:	Lucky Diamond Rich
Date:	2006
Place:	Australia

Tattooing every square inch of his body (plus his inner ears and gums) wasn't enough for Lucky Diamond Rich. When this Australian street performer completed his all-over ornamentation in 2004, he did the entire thing again, this time with black ink. Now he's going for a three-peat, adding white-inked areas with colorful designs on top (pictured). The **Most Tattooed Person** alive, Lucky Rich has spent over 1,000 hours being poked by the paint-bearing needles of tattoo artists. "I don't care what I get, how it looks, or who does it," he says with a colorful smile.

Tattoo Too

Body piercings take time to heal completely. Here are the recovery periods for some common procedures.

- Eyebrow: 1 – 3 months
- Earlobe: 3 – 4 months
- Nostril: 3 – 6 months
- Navel: 4 – 8 months

Tattoos don't vanish without help. Special lasers must be used to erase the ink from a person's skin. The lasers break down the tattoo ink, which is then absorbed by the body. Black, blue, purple, and red pigments break down easily. Yellow and green inks are harder to erase.

The art of tattooing began more than 5,000 years ago. The **Oldest Ice Body** of "Otzi" bears 57 tattoos on his preserved skin. Scientists date this find to be 5,300 years old!

ULTIMATE FACTS

The Polynesian word "tatau" means to mark or strike twice. The word "tattoo" is believed to have come from this combination. Tattooing can require two "hits" of ink, one for the design's outline and the second to fill in with color.

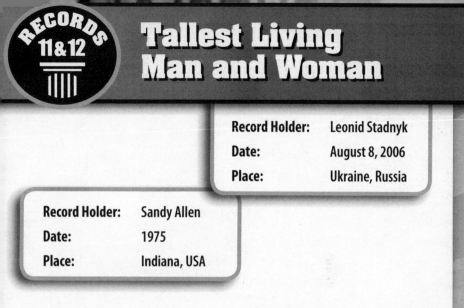

Record Holder:	Leonid Stadnyk
Date:	August 8, 2006
Place:	Ukraine, Russia

Record Holder:	Sandy Allen
Date:	1975
Place:	Indiana, USA

Talk about standing out in a crowd! Towering 8 feet, 5.5 inches above the ground, Leonid Stadnyk of Ukraine, Russia is the **Tallest Living Man**. Leonid's closest female competitor is Sandy Allen of Shelbyville, Indiana, USA. Standing 7 feet, 7.25 inches tall, Sandy has been the **Tallest Living Woman** since 1975. You might think Leonid and Sandy grew tall because of extra-sized genes — but you'd be wrong. Both of these record-breakers suffer from pituitary gigantism, a medical condition that causes the body to make too much growth hormone. Still, these two people enjoy their lives in spite of the difficulties caused by being bigger than the "average" sized person.

Sneak a peek into the lives of Sandy and Leonid on the next page!

Celebrations are for everyone, at any age or any size! On April 20, 2007, two famous ladies met over a slice of birthday cake. Sandy Allen traded stories of being a Guinness World Record-holder with Edna Parker, the **Oldest Living Person**, who had turned 114 years old (pictured).

ULTIMATE FACTS

Sandy Allen wears size 22 sneakers. She gets them from her friend, basketball player Rick "The Dunking Dutchman" Smits, who is 7 feet, 4 inches tall.

A brain operation at age 14 overstimulated Leonid Stadnyk's growth hormones. He hopes to follow in the footsteps of the previous record-holder, Xi Shun, who was married in 2007.

ULTIMATE FACTS

A certified veterinarian, Leonid Stadnyk had to quit his job after he discovered walking to work was the only method of transportation available to him. In March 2008, people gave Leonid the best gifts ever: a car and bicycle built just for him (pictured)!

Shortest Living Woman and Man

Record Holder:	Madge Bester
Date:	1999
Place:	South Africa

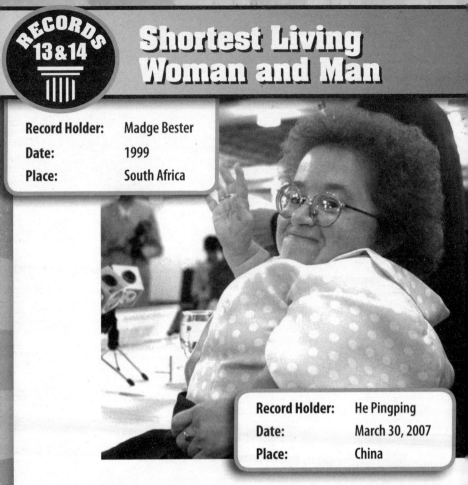

Record Holder:	He Pingping
Date:	March 30, 2007
Place:	China

The smallest adult humans on Earth could reach only to the kneecaps of the tallest ones! The **Shortest Living Woman**, Madge Bester of South Africa, has a height of 25.5 inches (pictured). Madge cannot grow any taller because of a deformed skeleton. She inherited this condition from her mother, who herself is only 27.5 inches tall. On March 30, 2007, doctors called endocrinologists — those who study the effects of hormones upon the body — gathered in China to officially measure He Pingping. The newest **Shortest Living Man** measures 2 feet 5.23 inches high.

Verne Troyer, who has acted in the Harry Potter and Austin Powers film series, is the **Shortest Adult Actor in a Supporting Role** at 2 feet 8 inches tall.

Making It Official

Not every extremely sized body makes it into the record books. The world's tallest and shortest people didn't automatically receive Guinness World Records. Contenders are measured under carefully controlled conditions to earn this honor. This process is called accreditation. Highlights from the official guidelines for being verified as the **Shortest Living Man**: The person must be at least 18, and measured three times in one day while standing upright and lying down — in their bare feet!

ULTIMATE FACTS

In a 1998 press conference, Madge Bester spoke out on behalf of the handicapped. Her message was, "Take charge of your life. Forget your disabilities and use your abilities."

Youngest Astronaut

Record Holder:	Gherman Stepanovich Titov
Date:	August 6, 1961
Place:	Kazakhstan, Russia

These days, people can't become astronauts without years of education, work experience, and training. But in the early days of space exploration, there were no such requirements. You could say that Major Gherman Stepanovich Titov of the former USSR cut the line! Born on September 11, 1935, Gherman was chosen by the Soviet space program to fly the *Vostok 2* mission (pictured). The capsule was launched on August 6, 1961, a month before his 26th birthday. Gherman spent one full day in space, making 17 Earth orbits and becoming the **Youngest Astronaut** during his out-of-this-world trip.

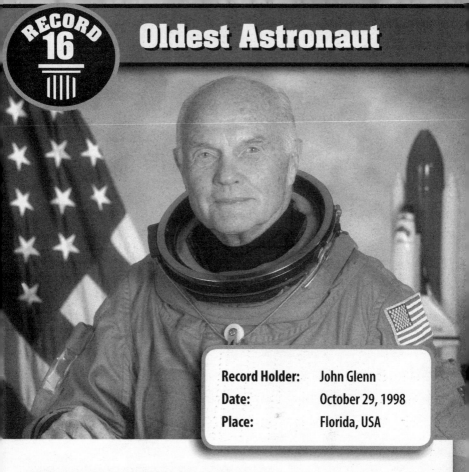

Record Holder:	John Glenn
Date:	October 29, 1998
Place:	Florida, USA

Add 52 candles to Gherman's cake and sing "Happy Birthday" to the granddaddy of all space explorers! Born on July 18, 1921, U.S. Senator John Glenn blasted into space on October 29, 1998, as part of the crew of *Discovery* STS-95. He was 77 years old at the time, making him by far the **Oldest Astronaut** (pictured). The nine-day trip was actually his second journey into space. John had been the first American astronaut to orbit the Earth way back in 1962. He suited up a second time to help scientists learn how space travel affected an older person.

Space Sick

Gherman Stepanovich Titov was not just the **Youngest Astronaut**. He was also the first person to suffer from space-adaptation syndrome, which is also known as space sickness. This condition is a type of motion sickness. Its symptoms include nausea, dizziness, headaches, and vomiting. It usually lasts from two to four days before an astronaut's body adapts to zero-gravity conditions. Space sickness is common. About 60 percent of all astronauts experience this syndrome during their first space journey.

John Glenn first entered space on February 20, 1962, as the pilot of a ship called *Friendship 7*. This mission made John the first American to achieve Earth orbit.

ULTIMATE FACTS

Former U.S. Senator Jake Garn had the worst case of space sickness on record. He was ill throughout the flight of the space shuttle *Discovery* from April 12–19, 1985.

WITH MAXIMUM EFFORT . . .

© Henry Boogert/www.boogertfotografie.nl

GUINNESS WORLD RECORDS™

MARATHON MAN

Before his swim through icy waters, Wim Hof meditates to prepare his body for shocking temperatures. Underwater, a guideline leads Wim between entry and exit holes cut into the frozen lake. Plunge into "Fantastic Feats" for more stories behind the headlines.

THESE ULTIMATE CHAMPIONS

© 2007 Ranald Mackechnie/Guinness World Records

BIG DREAMS
Gregory Dunham prepares for his next trip aboard his massive motorcycle "The Monster." How does he steer it? "Man Made" invites you along for the ride.

TUNE IT UP

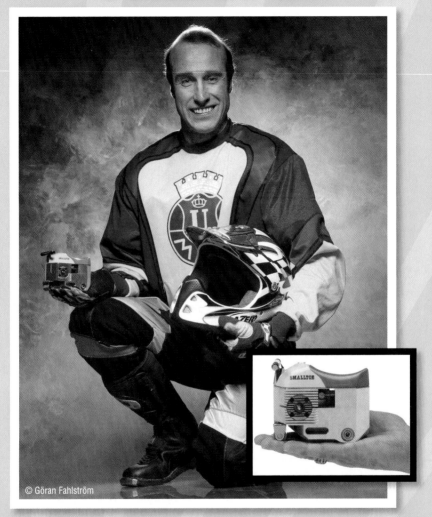

© Göran Fahlström

MIGHTY MINI

Tom Wiberg poses with his space-saving creation, "Smalltoe," a miniature motorcycle powered by a model airplane's engine. Can he ride his mini cycle? Consult "Man Made" for the details.

TEST ENDURANCE

© George H. H. Huey/Corbis

© Horizon International Images Limited/Alamy

DUNE DELIGHTS
Flowers bloom in the USA's Sonoran Desert as the **Wettest Desert**. Sand dunes flow among barren rocks in Mongolia's Gobi Desert, where the intense temperature range makes it the **Coldest Hot Desert**. Track the opposites around us in "Extremes of Nature."

DIVE DEEPER

© Max Gibbs/Oxford Scientific/Photolibrary

© Palm Beach Post

GO WITH THE FLOW

Being the **Slowest Fish** means a sea horse must know the best hiding spots, especially when dogs start scuba diving. Shadow the dog likes the ocean, but she won't explore outer space. That's another canine star. "Animals in Action" documents more daredevil acts by wildlife.

TURN HEADS

© BIOS/Peter Arnold Inc

THE MONKEY KING
One of the most colorful mammals, the male mandrill holds court in West Africa. Its opposite is found on the other side of the world. Sail between the extremes of species in "Creatures Big and Small."

OUTSHINE OTHERS

© Gareth Cattermole/Getty Images

GUINNESS WORLD RECORDS™

BLING BLISS
Body art has been practiced by many cultures for centuries. Elaine Davidson chose to express herself through pinning more than 2,000 pieces of jewelry into her skin. Find out more about body décor in "Fabulous Folks."

GROW TO GREAT LENGTHS

© PRNewsFoto/Guinness World Records 2008 Edition/Newscom

HORSE SENSE
Thumbelina and Radar, current record-holders in the under- and over-sized horse category, meet up in the paddock. Measure more wildlife records in "Creatures Big and Small."

...TO BE A GUINNESS WORLD RECORD-HOLDER!

CHAPTER 3

Extremes of Nature

This chapter let you experience some of our planet's dangerous extremes in the safety of your own home. Feel the warm rain in the world's wettest desert and the chill in the coldest wasteland anywhere. Plunge into the inky blackness of the deepest ocean trenches before climbing to the top of the highest mountain. Finally, put on your headphones and hear about the Earth's loudest and (shhhh!) quietest moments.

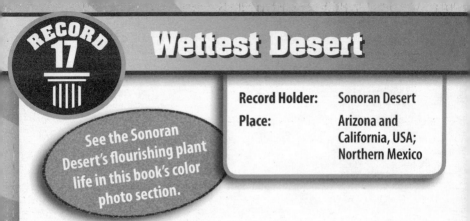

Wettest Desert

See the Sonoran Desert's flourishing plant life in this book's color photo section.

Record Holder: Sonoran Desert

Place: Arizona and California, USA; Northern Mexico

It seems odd to read the words "wettest" and "desert" in the same record title. An area is called a desert if it receives less than 8 inches of annual rainfall, with its rate of water evaporation greater than its precipitation amounts. The Sonoran Desert's yearly rainfall averages between 4.7 to 11.8 inches — just enough to earn this hot spot the Guinness World Records title of **Wettest Desert**. Covering parts of Arizona and California, USA, plus northern Mexico, the Sonoran hits daytime temperatures of up to 104 degrees Fahrenheit in the summer. The region experiences two wet seasons annually, one from December to March, and another from July to September.

ULTIMATE FACTS

Thanks to its rainy seasons, the Sonoran Desert is full of life. This area is home to 60 mammal species, 350 bird species, 20 amphibian species, and more than 100 reptile species. It also boasts more than 2,000 types of plants.

Coldest Desert

Record Holder:	McMurdo Dry Valleys
Place:	Antarctica

Let's visit the chilly desert without getting frostbite. This photo is a bird's-eye view of the peaks of the Royal Society Range located in Taylor Valley, one of the three main valleys of the McMurdo's Dry Valleys region.

Planning a visit to Antarctica's McMurdo Dry Valleys? Leave your raincoat behind. This arid area gets less than 4 inches of precipitation per year, so you have almost no chance of getting wet. You will, however, get awfully chilly if you don't bundle up! The average annual temperature in the Dry Valleys is -4 degrees Fahrenheit. That might sound cold, but it's actually balmy compared to nearby area lows of -85 degrees. That frigid temperature is enough to freeze your skin instantly — and, incidentally, to earn this region the title of **Coldest Desert** in the world (pictured).

A real place of contradictions is the Gobi Desert in Central Asia. Summer temperatures reach 104 degrees F. Wintertime shivers at -4 degrees F. This means the Gobi is the record-holder for **Coldest Hot Desert.** See the Gobi's scorching sand dunes in this book's special color photo section.

ULTIMATE FACTS

What could live on the ice and rocky soil of Antarctica's McMurdo Dry Valleys? Algae, nematode worms, phytoplankton and bacteria thrive there. Scientists believe that conditions in McMurdo may be similar to those on Mars. By studying this area, they hope to learn about possible life forms on other planets.

Deepest Ocean Trench

Record Holder:	Mariana Trench
Date:	1951
Place:	Western Pacific Ocean

Imagine you could pick up the **Highest Mountain** (see Record 20), turn it upside down, and poke it into the Mariana Trench. When you were done, there would be 1.3 *miles* of water covering the mountain's base! Located in the Pacific Ocean near Guam, the **Deepest Ocean Trench** plunges 6.8 miles below sea level. Only two people have ever visited this remote spot. Traveling in a small submersible, scientists Jacques Piccard and Don Walsh reached the trench floor on January 23, 1960. They spent only 20 minutes in the trench's pitch-dark depths before starting the three-hour journey back to the surface.

ULTIMATE FACTS

At the bottom of the Mariana Trench, the water pressure is more than 1,000 times greater than the air pressure at sea level. This force would instantly squash unprotected human lungs and other gas-filled organs. It would have no effect, however, on muscles and other liquid-based tissues.

Highest Mountain

Record Holder:	Mount Everest
Date:	1852
Place:	Nepal and Tibet

You're in for quite a hike if you want to enjoy the view from the top of Mount Everest (pictured). Located in the Himalayan range, this massive mountain juts 29,035 feet (more than 5½ miles) above sea level. That's higher than any other peak on the planet! Many people dream of conquering this giant, and a good number have actually done it. As of 2007, a total of 2,436 individuals had stood on Everest's peak. The climb is hard and sometimes lethal. Yet many people think the journey to the **Highest Mountain** is worth the risk.

ULTIMATE FACTS

At the top of Mount Everest, the air is thin. It contains only about one-third as much oxygen as sea-level air. That's barely enough oxygen to support human life! For this reason, most climbers carry bottled oxygen when they attempt to reach Everest's summit.

The mountain also holds another record that climbers heed as a warning before making their attempt. The **Most Deaths on Mount Everest in One Day** occurred on May 10, 1996. A late-afternoon blizzard stranded climbers near the treacherous top. It was too late for eight members of the group, in spite of a daring helicopter rescue.

Loudest Noise

Record Holder:	Eruption of Krakatoa
Date:	August 27, 1883
Place:	Sunda Strait, Indonesia

If your parents dislike loud music, imagine what they would say about a sound that could be heard around the world! The **Loudest Noise** in recorded history rocked the Earth on August 27, 1883, when an Indonesian volcano named Krakatoa (locally known as "Krakatua") erupted with the force of 26 hydrogen bombs. The sound from this event rippled outward in all directions, eventually reaching the ears of people living nearly 3,100 miles away. At this point, the noise sounded like distant cannons. Up close, however, it was much worse. The explosion destroyed the volcano, and the hearing ability of anyone within 100 miles.

ULTIMATE FACTS

Since 1927, a new volcano named Anak Krakatau ("child of Krakatau") has been spewing gas, hot rocks, and ash. Because of these deposits, the volcano grows about 5 inches per week.

Quietest Place on Earth

Record Holder:	Anechoic Test Chamber at Orfield Laboratories
Date:	January 21, 2004
Place:	Minnesota, USA

Are your ears ringing? Let's take things down a few decibels with a visit to the Anechoic Test Chamber at Orfield Laboratories in Minneapolis, Minnesota, USA (pictured). Certified by Guinness World Records as the **Quietest Place on Earth**, this chamber absorbs sound waves instead of letting them bounce around. The result is a sound level as low as -9.4 decibels (dB), far below the human hearing threshold of 0 dB. People who have visited this chamber report a silence so deep that you can hear your heart beat and your blood pound. The experience is "a bit unnerving," whispered one visitor.

How Loud?

Every noise has a decibel rating. This list ranks everyday sounds.

- Near total silence ......0 dB
- Quiet library ....30 dB
- Moderate rainfall .....50 dB
- Conversation............60 dB
- Vacuum cleaner........70 dB
- Alarm clock ....80 dB
- Lawnmower..............90 dB
- Chainsaw ....100 dB
- Rock concert ....120 dB
- Jet engine..............140 dB
- Permanent hearing damage ..... Above 140 dB
- Whistles by the blue whale ....188 dB

CHAPTER 4

Animals in Action

Animals do amazing things, and here are some records to prove it! In this chapter, you'll leap for joy with some bouncy beasts and plummet into the ocean with an unusual dog. While you're wet, let's take a swim with the world's fastest and slowest fish, then dodge history's deadliest crocodile attack. It's an action-packed celebration of the world's wildlife.

First Dog in Space

Record Holder:	Laika
Date:	November 3, 1957
Place:	Kazakhstan, Russia

The Soviet space program went to the dogs on November 3, 1957, when a stray pooch named Laika was launched into Earth orbit aboard the *Sputnik 2* spacecraft (pictured). Nicknamed "Muttnik" by the media, this mission made Laika famous around the world as the **First Dog in Space**. Sadly, Laika did not survive her history-making journey. She did, however, prove that it was possible for a living passenger to reach space orbit and endure weightlessness. By doing this, the pioneering pup paved the way for other animals — and humans — to blast off with better results. Today, modern spaceflights often carry animal passengers. In 2003, the space shuttle *Columbia* carried silkworms, spiders, bees, ants, and Japanese killfish along with seven human astronauts. These weren't the astronauts' pets along for a ride. They were the subjects of important scientific experiments on space's effect upon different species.

Deepest Scuba Dive By a Dog

Record Holder:	Shadow
Date:	2002
Place:	Grand Cayman Island

Like Laika, a dog named Shadow knows a few things about exceeding expectations. This retriever/ Labrador mix regularly scuba dives with her owner, Dwayne Folsom, off the coast of Grand Cayman Island. The pair usually descend to around 13 feet, which is the **Deepest Scuba Dive By a Dog** on record. When diving, Shadow wears a specially adapted suit that includes a helmet, a weighted jacket, and a breathing tube connected to her owner's air tank. She leaves her leash and collar at home while taking her incredible underwater walks. See Shadow and Dwayne in action in this book's color photo section.

Not all dogs like water, but some breeds love taking the plunge! Labradors and golden retrievers are "water dogs." Shadow is a mixture of these two swim-sational breeds, so it's no wonder she took to scuba diving like a duck — or, in this case, a dog — to water!

RECORD 25

Fastest Fish

Record Holder:	Cosmopolitan sailfish
Date:	1999
Place:	Florida, USA

The fastest human swimmers can reach speeds of approximately 5 miles per hour. That's quick for a person — but compared to the world's **Fastest Fish**, it's the aquatic equivalent of a leisurely Sunday stroll! The swiftest swimmer on the planet is the cosmopolitan sailfish *(Istiophorus platypterus)*, an 11-foot game fish found in warm waters around the world (pictured). In a series of speed trials carried out at Long Key Fishing Camp in Florida, USA, this ocean Olympian took out 300 feet of line in 3 seconds. That's equal to a velocity of 68 miles per hour. Hey, watch the speed limit!

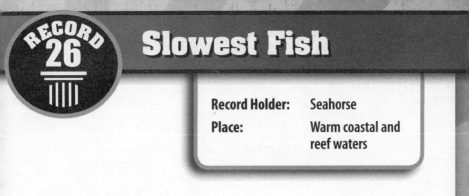

Record Holder: Seahorse

Place: Warm coastal and reef waters

While the sailfish zips past overhead, the slow-moving seahorse (family *Syngnathidas)* takes it easy on the ocean floor. This fragile looking and variously colored fish spends its life clinging to seaweed, coral, and other underwater anchors. It moves around by fluttering its tiny fins. This swimming technique can work in a pinch, but it sure isn't quick. It would take about five minutes for a medium-size seahorse to swim from one end of a bathtub to the other! Don't call this little critter lazy. It can't move any faster because its rigid body structure makes the seahorse a natural at being the **Slowest Fish**.

See the range of camouflage colors a seahorse can be in this book's special color photo section.

Like sailfish, seahorses have dorsal fins on their backs. The seahorse's dorsal fin is small and transparent. The dorsal fin is supported by delicate spines that can move independently. The seahorse uses these spines to flap the dorsal fin and push itself forward through the water.

Dorsal Fin

The huge sail of the sailfish is actually a modified dorsal (back) fin. Under normal conditions, the sailfish folds this mighty fin down. It raises the fin when it feels threatened. This tactic makes the fish look much bigger than it really is. Sailfish may also use their dorsal fins as barriers to herd schools of fish or squid into small, yummy groups perfectly sized for eating.

Most Dangerous Mosquito

Record Holder:	*Anopheles* mosquito
Date:	Since the beginning of recorded history
Place:	Worldwide

How scary could a tiny *Anopheles* mosquito be (pictured)? Scientists estimate that this 0.1-inch critter has probably caused half of all natural human deaths since the Stone Age! It reached this deadly tally during its daily feedings. After the mosquito takes a "bite," it injects a malaria-causing parasite into its human victims' bloodstreams. Malaria is a devastating and often fatal disease. Each year in sub-Saharan Africa alone, up to 2.8 million people die from malaria, making the *Anopheles* the **Most Dangerous Mosquito** — not to mention the most harmful animal of any type — alive on our planet today.

Most Fatalities in a Crocodile Attack

Record Holder:	Saltwater crocodile
Date:	February 19–20, 1945
Place:	Ramree Island, Burma

One of the most horrifying battles of World War II was fought against an enemy feared by all humans around the world — the saltwater crocodile (pictured). On the night of February 19, 1945, a Japanese Army unit found itself trapped by the British Navy on the Burmese (now Myanmar) island of Ramree. The Japanese soldiers fled through a swamp, not realizing that it was infested with 15-foot-long saltwater crocodiles (Crocodylus porosus). By morning, only 20 of the original 1,000 soldiers were alive. Hungry reptiles had eaten the other 980 men, chomping their way to the **Most Fatalities in a Crocodile Attack** in recorded history.

The estuarine or saltwater crocodile is the **Largest Crocodile** in the world, capable of growing more than 20 feet in length. The Greeks named these giants after their much smaller lizard cousin, the *krokodelios*. Perhaps it was meant as a joke, but you'll stop laughing if these crocodiles smile at you.

Bearing up to 68 sharp teeth, a saltwater crocodile is certain to be noticed when it latches onto its prey. Crocodiles chomp their mighty jaws shut with a force of 5,000 pounds per square inch. That's more than 10 times the power of a great white shark!

Highest Jump By a Horse

Record Holder:	Huaso
Date:	February 5, 1949
Place:	Santiago, Chile

Many horses are good jumpers, but one is definitely a leap above the rest! On February 5, 1949, a horse named Huaso (formerly Faithful) carried rider Alberto Larraguibel Morales over an 8-foot, 1.25-inch barrier at the Vina del Mar showgrounds in Santiago, Chile. After reaching the other side, Huaso earned the Guinness World Record for the **Highest Jump By a Horse** (pictured). Since 1949, many attempts have been made to break this record, but none have succeeded. Huaso's accomplishment stands to this day as one of the longest-running unbroken records in sports history.

RECORD 30
Highest Jump By a Pig

Record Holder: Kotetsu
Date: August 22, 2004
Place: Mie, Japan

A jumping horse is a common sight. But a leaping pig? Now *that's* a surprise! The title of **Highest Jump By a Pig** belongs to a pot-bellied porker named Kotetsu (pictured). The soaring swine earned his record on August 22, 2004, after he cleared a 27.5-inch obstacle at the Mokumoku Tedsukuri Farm in Mie, Japan. That might not sound high, but it's a tall order for an animal whose stomach hangs close to the ground. There's no doubt Kotetsu went above and beyond the call of piggie duty with his record-breaking jump!

A Real Cinderella Story

A dog named Cindy knows a thing or two about jumping. Officially named "Cinderella May a Holly Grey," this greyhound showed a natural leaping ability when she was just a puppy. Cindy's owners, Kate Long and Kathleen Conroy of Florida, USA, set up practice fences for their pooch. By mid-2003, Cindy was ready to quit practicing and hit the big time! On October 4, 2003, Cindy leaped a barrier of 66 inches to earn the Guinness World Record for **Highest Jump By a Dog** (pictured). Three years later, she broke her own record with a jump of 68 inches!

Cindy competed in dog agility trials before earning her title. In these events, doggie athletes navigate obstacles such as seesaws, tunnels, poles, and fences.

CHAPTER 5

Man Made

If one person can build it, another person can construct it better! That's the theme of this chapter, where we get up close and personal with some of mankind's most extreme creations. Put the largest motorcycles, cars, and submarines in gear before scaling down with the smallest models. You'll also traverse the world's deepest tunnel and cross its highest bridge. It's a showcase of building excess . . . and Guinness World Records success!

Smallest Motorcycle

Record Holder:	*Smalltoe*
Date:	2003
Place:	Sweden

In most U.S. states, you must be at least 16 years old to lawfully operate a motorcycle. Some states give motorcycle learner's permits starting at age 15.

They say, "good things come in small packages," and a mini machine named *Smalltoe* proves it! Tom Wiberg of Sweden built this tiny two-wheeler in 2003. The **Smallest Motorcycle** ever made, *Smalltoe*'s wheels are just 3.14 inches apart, and its seat is a mere 2.55 inches — about the height of a matchbox — off the ground. How do you ride it? Not the usual way. Tom carefully puts one foot on the seat then balances constantly while the cycle races forward at its top speed — of 1.2 miles per hour! See Tom steering *Smalltoe* in this book's color photo section.

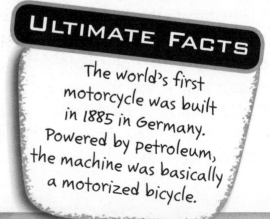

ULTIMATE FACTS

The world's first motorcycle was built in 1885 in Germany. Powered by petroleum, the machine was basically a motorized bicycle.

RECORD 32

Tallest Rideable Motorcycle

Record Holder:	*The Monster*
Date:	2005
Place:	California, USA

See *The Monster* featured in this book's color photo section!

You'd need to stack 53 *Smalltoes* on top of each other to equal the height of the **Tallest Rideable Motorcycle**. Built by Gregory Dunham of Stockton, California, USA, *The Monster* is 11 feet, 3 inches tall, and 20 feet, 4 inches long. It rolls from place to place on two, 3-foot-wide tires at speeds up to 65 miles per hour. It took Gregory three and a half years with $300,000 to finalize his creation. Why did he do it? "Because everyone said I could not, and it was my dream," says Gregory. "ALL things are possible to those who believe!" The name of another one of Gregory's super-sized motorcycles: *Dream Big*.

Motorcycle Madness

Motorcycle enthusiasts of all shapes and sizes gather every summer in Sturgis, South Dakota, for the world's largest bike event. Held in August, the Sturgis Motorcycle Rally attracts more than 500,000 people — most of them on motorcycles — each year. That's a lot of visitors to Sturgis, which has a year-round population of just 6,700. But the influx is fine with the town leaders, who call their home the "City of Riders." "What used to be just a gathering of people is now an economic event," said Maury LaRue, the city's mayor, in a 2007 interview.

Smallest Production Car

Record Holder:	Peel *P50*
Date:	1962
Place:	Isle of Man, UK

Here's a record that will ap-PEEL to auto enthusiasts! Measuring 53 inches long, 39 inches wide, and 53 inches high, the Peel *P50* is the **Smallest Production Car** ever produced. Fifty of these mini machines were built by the Manx Peel Engineering Company on the Isle of Man, UK, between 1962 and 1965. Designed to carry one person plus a shopping bag, the *P50* had no reverse gear. To make tight turns, a driver had to get out of the car and rotate the 130-pound vehicle by hand (pictured).

Longest Car

Tight turns are a challenge for most vehicles, but there's a secret to it if you're driving the **Longest Car** (pictured). Built by Jay Ohrberg of Burbank, California, USA, the *American Dream* has 26 wheels, and measures 100 feet from bumper to bumper. The lengthiest limo on the planet is hinged in the middle for it to bend around corners. A modified 1980 Cadillac, Jay's creation was designed for looks, not comfort. Translation: This Caddy has no passenger seating. You'll feel every bump in the road when you embark on this *loooong* ride!

Record Holder:	*American Dream*
Date:	1999
Place:	California, USA

Despite its lack of seats, Jay Ohrberg's *American Dream* has some amazing features inside its impressive frame. The large limo features a king-size waterbed, a swimming pool with a diving board, and a helicopter-landing pad for more travel options.

Largest Submarine

Record Holder:	941 Akula (Typhoon)
Date:	September 23, 1980
Place:	Severodvinsk, Russia

Typhoon-class submarines are designed to hide underwater for long periods. A fully loaded 941 Akula can easily stay submerged for six months or longer without surfacing for supplies.

When a submarine drops below the surface, it pushes water aside. The bigger the sub's size, the bigger the displacement of water. By this measure, a Russian rover called the 941 Akula, or "Typhoon" class, is the **Largest Submarine** ever built. First launched on September 23, 1980, at a secret shipyard in Severodvinsk, Russia, this vast vessel displaces 58 million pounds (26,500 tons) of seawater when fully submerged (pictured). It measures 562 feet, 7 inches from stem to stern, and can house a crew of 160 people. A lot of sub needs a lot of sailors!

Smallest Submarine

Record Holder:	*BIG*
Date:	June 26, 2005
Place:	Quebec, Canada

Not all submarines are military monsters. Many are one-person vehicles, or personal submersibles nicknamed P-subs, built by blowtorch-wielding amateurs in their garages. That's the story behind *BIG*, the mini-machine that holds the Guinness World Record for **Smallest Submarine** (pictured). Built by Pierre Poulin of Canada, *BIG* displaces just 1,366 pounds of water. That's less than one *forty-thousandth* of the Akula's volume! Pierre took his handcrafted creation for its first official dive in Lake Memphremagog in Magog, Quebec, Canada, on June 26, 2005. P-subs aren't built for depth or long voyages because they are small and leaky. Pierre noticed two leaks during his submersion. He grabbed paper towels, reached a depth of 10 feet, then safely resurfaced.

Deepest Road Tunnel

Record Holder:	Hitra Tunnel
Date:	December 1994
Place:	Between the mainland and Hitra, Norway

You don't need a submarine to travel safely through Norway's underwater Hitra Tunnel. This three-lane, 3.5-mile-long passage plunges to depths of 866 feet below sea level, making it the **Deepest Road Tunnel** ever built. Opened in December 1994, the record-breaking road links the Norwegian mainland with the island of Hitra, which has just 4,100 residents. Why did engineers go to such lengths — and mind-boggling depths — for such a small group of people? Observers say it has to do with Norway's fiercely independent culture. "Norwegians like to feel free, and today, thanks to the tunnel, we feel free 24 hours a day," said one happy Hitran resident.

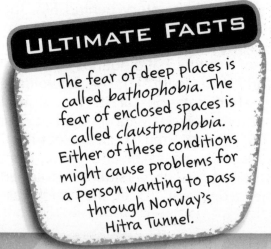

ULTIMATE FACTS

The fear of deep places is called *bathophobia*. The fear of enclosed spaces is called *claustrophobia*. Either of these conditions might cause problems for a person wanting to pass through Norway's Hitra Tunnel.

Highest Suspension Bridge

Record Holder:	Royal Gorge Bridge
Date:	November 1929
Place:	Colorado, USA

Feeling a little closed-in after your underwater drive? Then take a breath of fresh air on the Royal Gorge Bridge near Cañon City, Colorado, USA. The **Highest Suspension Bridge** in the world, this airy overpass spans the Colorado River at a dizzying height of 1,053 feet above water level (pictured). The super structure was built from June through November 1929 as a tourist attraction. Today, the bridge still serves its original purpose. Thousands of people walk its wooden planks each year to get an eagle's-eye view of Colorado's stunning scenery.

ULTIMATE FACTS

Some people suffer from a condition called *gephyrophobia*, which means "fear of bridges." These people are not necessarily afraid of the bridge itself. They worry that they will have a panic attack during a crossing and become so ill that they won't be able to continue.

CHAPTER 6

Fantastic Feats

Through effort or accident, humans have achieved tremendous things — and Guinness World Records has chronicled them! In this chapter, you'll become a human ice cube during a chilly swim before thawing out on a long-distance firewalk. Shoot arrows into the air, then pluck them right out again . . . by hand. Help yourself to some tasty pizza-related tidbits before you meet the ultimate survivalists. No matter how you slice it, this information is sure to satisfy your craving for ultimate records!

Longest Swim Under Ice with Breath Held

Record Holder:	Wim Hof
Date:	March 16, 2000
Place:	Kolari, Finland

Nicknamed the "Iceman," Wim Hof of the Netherlands relies on a mental technique called Inner Fire to control his body's reaction to cold (see Wim mediating in this book's color photo section). After mediating, Wim completed a swim of 188.6 feet beneath three feet of ice near Kolari, Finland, on March 16, 2000. The water temperature at the time was a sub-freezing 21.2 degrees Fahrenheit — *brrrr*! Most people would die under those conditions. The frost-proof Wim, however, wore nothing but a regular swimsuit and goggles while successfully completing the **Longest Swim Under Ice with Breath Held**.

Farthest Distance Fire Walking

Record Holder:	Trever McGhee
Date:	November 9, 2007
Place:	Alberta, Canada

This photo documents the first of Trever McGhee's three record attempts. Here he only made it to 50 feet before leaping clear from the coals because it was too hot-Hot-HOT!

Have you ever singed your soles on a sandy beach in the summertime? Think about that discomfort, then compare it to the heat endured by Trever McGhee, a motivational speaker who holds the title of **Farthest Distance Fire Walking** (pictured). On November 9, 2007, Trever "hot-footed it" over 597 feet of smoldering embers with a temperature of 1,214 to 1,307 degrees Fahrenheit. The incredible "feet" was part of an ABC-TV special filmed at Symons Valley Rodeo Grounds in Calgary, Alberta, Canada.

Even Trever McGhee burns his feet when fire walking. He calls the burns "fire kisses."

Firewalking 101

Most firewalks are done over coals that measure more than 1,000 degrees Fahrenheit. Too hot? Consider these sizzling facts:

1. The coals are usually covered with ash. The ash layer blocks much of the coals' heat.
2. Only a tiny bit of the foot touches the coals at any moment.
3. The firewalker moves quickly to minimize his or her skin's contact with the coals.
4. Water and blood take time to absorb heat and change temperature.

Between points 1, 2, 3, and 4, experts say that it is difficult for a person to get burned on a short firewalk — *if* he or she walks fast. A long walk, however, is a different story. There would be some "blistered soles"! OUCH!

Fastest Time to Shoot 10 Arrows

Record Holder:	Luis Caídas Martín
Date:	June 4, 2006
Place:	Madrid, Spain

When Luis Caídas Martín shoots to win, he really hits the target! A practiced archer, Martín shot 10 arrows in 1 minute, 7 seconds on the set of *Guinness World Records — El Show de los Records* in Madrid, Spain, on June 4, 2006. That's the **Fastest Time to Shoot 10 Arrows** ever recorded. For each shot, Luis had to pick up an arrow, nock it onto the bowstring, raise and draw the bow, and take aim before releasing his grip. That's a lot to accomplish in six seconds, but Luis was more than up to the record-worthy challenge.

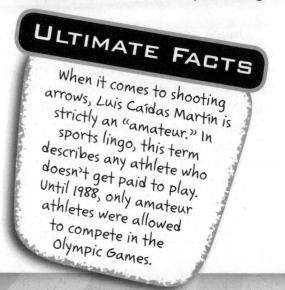

ULTIMATE FACTS

When it comes to shooting arrows, Luis Caídas Martín is strictly an "amateur." In sports lingo, this term describes any athlete who doesn't get paid to play. Until 1988, only amateur athletes were allowed to compete in the Olympic Games.

Record Holder:	Anthony Kelly
Date:	December 15, 2006
Place:	Beijing, China

Unlike target competitions, arrow-catching isn't an Olympic sport. But if it were, Anthony Kelly of Australia would definitely earn the gold medal! Standing at a distance of 26 feet from two archers, Anthony successfully caught 36 separate arrows shot in two minutes (pictured). This fantastic feat occurred in Beijing, China, on December 15, 2006. It wasn't the first time Anthony had made the record books. This attempt broke his previous Guinness World Record (which had stood at 34) for **Arrows Caught By Hand in Two Minutes**. Billed as "The Reaction Man™," Anthony practices his lickety-split reflexes every day as a martial artist and a professional Reaction Training coach.

Most Pizzas Made in One Hour

Record Holder:	Kevin Schroeder
Date:	May 4, 2003
Place:	Maryland, USA

Smile and say "Cheese!" The mozzarella was in motion on May 4, 2003, when Kevin Schroeder went after the Guinness World Record for **Most Pizzas Made in One Hour**. Working at Perry's Pizzeria in Middle River, Maryland, USA, Kevin tossed dough, spread sauce, and sprinkled shredded cheese for 60 solid minutes. When the timer sounded, Kevin had cranked out 93 pies. That's about one pizza every 39 seconds. All those pizza chains that guarantee 30-minute service can talk to this pie-riffic pro!

ULTIMATE FACTS

The **Most Expensive Pizza** at $178 is served at Gordon Ramsey's Maze restaurant in London, UK!

Fastest Time to Eat a 12-Inch Pizza

Record Holder:	Tom Waes
Date:	December 2, 2006
Place:	Ghent, Belgium

Tom Waes of Belgium probably couldn't beat Kevin Schroeder in a pizza-making contest. When it comes to consuming pizza, however, there's no doubt that Tom is the big cheese! This amazing eater displayed his skills on December 2, 2006, when he gobbled down a 12-inch pie in 2 minutes, 19.91 seconds — the **Fastest Time to Eat a 12-Inch Pizza** ever recorded. Tom didn't stuff the slice into his mouth. He used a knife and fork to cut it into bite-sized chunks first. Imagine how fast he might have been if he had neglected his table manners!

Tastiest Take-Out Ever

On June 8, 2006, Papa John's pizza chain made the **Largest Pizza Delivery** with 13,500 piping-hot pies to the NASSCO shipyard in San Diego, California, USA. NASSCO dialed up the super-sized order as a reward for its 6,000 employees, who had just finished building a U.S. Navy ship (USNS Lewis and Clark auxiliary ship). It took 100 Papa John's employees a total of five hours to prepare the pizzas, which were delivered in 20 oven-equipped vans.

Deepest Underwater Escape Without Equipment

Record Holder:	Richard A. Slater
Date:	September 28, 1970
Place:	California, USA

When Richard A. Slater woke up on September 28, 1970, he had no idea he would be a Guinness World Record-holder by the end of the day! Richard was operating a small submarine called the *Nekton Beta* off the California coast when a sunken powerboat rammed his craft. The *Beta*'s port shattered and the submarine sank to the sea floor, 225 feet below. Semiconscious, Richard managed to squeeze out of the water-filled sub and float to the ocean surface. Miraculously, he survived his ordeal, earning the record for **Deepest Underwater Escape Without Equipment** in the process.

ULTIMATE FACTS

Richard A. Slater was exposed to crushing water pressure during his underwater escape. This pressure ruptured both of his eardrums.

Highest Fall Survived Without a Parachute

Record Holder:	Vesna Vulovic
Date:	January 26, 1972
Place:	Czechoslovakia

A person falling from a height of 225 feet — the distance swum by Richard A. Slater during his great escape — would almost surely be killed. Yet the **Highest Fall Survived Without a Parachute** is nearly 150 times that extreme! On January 26, 1972, flight attendant Vesna Vulovic plummeted 6.3 miles inside the wreckage of a bomb-damaged airplane. She suffered a fractured skull, two broken legs, and three broken vertebrae when the plane cashed into a Czechoslovakian mountain. Unlike the other 27 people on the flight, Vesna lived to tell the miraculous tale of her survival.

ULTIMATE FACTS

Vesna Vulovic returned to her job after recovering from her fantastic fall. She continued flying for 18 more years, without another Guinness World Record-worthy incident.

Extreme Survival

People can live through some truly incredible events. Straight from the Guinness World Records archives, here are some other extreme situations that people have survived.

- Being struck by lightning — seven times!

- Drifting at sea for 484 days — that's 16 months!

- A cardiac arrest — of more than four hours!

- A 75-story drop — in a broken elevator!

- A motorcycle crash — at 200 miles per hour!

- A car crash — at 360 miles per hour!

- A body temperature — of only 57.5 degrees Fahrenheit!

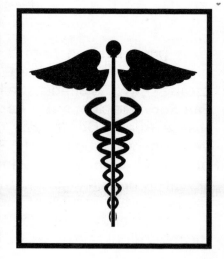

CONCLUSION

Extreme-ly Satisfying!

Although our thrill ride is over, your exploration of the world's most extreme animals, people, and stories doesn't have to be. Go exploring among the online archives *(www.guinnessworldrecords.com)* and within the pages of *Guinness World Records* at your local library or bookstore. You're guaranteed to find thousands of records covering all things big, small, long, short, least, most, and many other sensational superlatives.

Interested in making history by having your own record? Check out the official guidelines on how to become a record-breaker featured on the next page. Maybe your name will appear in the next edition of the record books!

BE A RECORD-BREAKER!

Message from the Keeper of the Records:

Record-breakers are the ultimate in one way or another — the youngest, the oldest, the tallest, the smallest. So how do you get to be a record-breaker? Follow these important steps:

1. Before you attempt your record, check with us to make sure your record is suitable and safe. Get your parents' permission. Next, contact one of our officials by using the record application form at *www.guinnessworldrecords.com*.

2. Tell us about your idea. Give us as much information as you can, including what the record is, when you want to attempt it, where you'll be doing it, and other relevant information.

a) We will tell you if a record already exists, what safety guidelines you must follow during your attempt to break that record, and what evidence we need as proof that you completed your attempt.

b) If your idea is a brand-new record nobody has set yet, we need to make sure it meets our requirements. If it does, then we'll write official rules and safety guidelines specific to that record idea and make sure all attempts are made in the same way.

3. Whether it is a new or existing record, we will send you the guidelines for your selected record. Once you receive these, you can make your attempt at any time. You do not need a Guinness World Record official at your attempt. But you do need to gather evidence. Find out more about the kind of evidence we need to see by visiting our website.

4. Think you've already set or broken a record? Put all of your evidence as specified by the guidelines in an envelope and mail it to us at Guinness World Records.

5. Our officials will investigate your claim fully — a process that can take a few weeks, depending on the number of claims we've received and how complex your record is.

6. If you're successful, you will receive an official certificate that says you are now a Guinness World Record-holder!

Need more info? Check out *www.guinnessworldrecords.com* for lots more hints, tips, and some top record ideas. Good luck!

PHOTO CREDITS